To Love and Serve

Jonathan Draper is Canon Theologian of York Minster and Diocesan Advisor for Ministerial Development. He was born and brought up in the USA, coming to the UK to undertake his doctoral studies at the University of Durham. He trained for ordination at Ripon College Cuddesdon, where he then taught from 1985 to 1992, and served as Vicar of Putney in Southwark Diocese from 1992 to 2000. He is married with three children.

To Love and Serve

Being the Body of Christ
in a Time of Change

Jonathan Draper

Published in Great Britain in 2003
Society for Promoting Christian Knowledge
Holy Trinity Church
Marylebone Road
London NW1 4DU

British Library Cataloguing-in-Publication Data

A catalogue record for this book is available from the British Library

ISBN 0-281-05540-8

1 3 5 7 9 10 8 6 4 2

Typeset by WestKey Ltd, Falmouth, Cornwall
Printed in Great Britain by Bookmarque Ltd, Croydon, Surrey

Contents

Introduction

This is a book about being the Body of Christ in a context of change. Part of the argument of the book is that we become the Body of Christ as we attend properly to God. The other part of the argument is that we attend properly to God in a context of change when we pay proper attention to the changes. The first six chapters focus on the first part of the argument: how do we become the Body of Christ?

Chapter 7 is different. In it I have picked up a theme – change – which recurs in the first six chapters without really being thoroughly explored. It seems to me that change is of such fundamental importance to Christians today, and is so widely feared and misunderstood, that it merits a separate and longer treatment. I also think that the examination of change helps to flesh out some of the material in the previous six chapters, and provides something of the context for understanding them

More than that stands behind the writing of this book. The churches (not least the Church of England from which I am writing) are going through a time of some turmoil. In almost all the churches, established patterns of ministry are under great strain and in some places collapsing. Financial pressures are driving organizational, institutional and educational changes. The morale among increasing numbers of the full-time stipendiary clergy is low. A whole host of responses – sometimes pulling in different directions – are being made to this turmoil in different parts of the UK and sometimes within different parts of a denomination. Part of what I hope to achieve with this book is a fresh look at the basics: what does it mean to attend to God? What does it mean to explore our faith? What does it mean to engage with the world? What does it mean today to be the Body of Christ in the world? And perhaps the most difficult of all, how are we to understand and handle change?

I offer what is here as a contribution to thinking through some of these issues. I hope, however, that no one will be deceived by the relative gentleness of the approach; simply wishing to contribute to a debate is not the whole point. For I feel some real urgency about these issues as well. There is an opportunity in our times and context for shedding some of the less helpful baggage we carry from our past; baggage that I think stands in the way of mission. We have no choice but to think creatively if we are to take on the turmoil and come out the other side of it as stronger and more focussed churches. The alternative is simply continuing our drift off into final irrelevance.

I, for one, would not like to see that happen. While many a prophetic voice has been raised in the churches over the past 20 or 30 years warning that changes were needed, they have not, by and large, been listened to; reports have been noted and then quietly shelved; alarm bells have been rung and then simply shut off. We can't do that now. The pressures are too great and the world changing too fast for us to dither. Creative refocussing of our resources and energies is needed now.

This book, however, is not going to solve the problems. What I hope it will do is point at least in the direction in which some of those changes need to be made. Perhaps I am suggesting in this book some of the principles we need in order to effect the changes that are to come, whether we like them or not.

That's all this book is about. It does not suggest a radical reorganization of the Church, new forms of ministry, or even 'new ways of being church'. It is, rather, an attempt to get us to take the foundations of our faith more seriously as the way to address the needs of our times and context.

The first six chapters of this book first saw the light of day, in a slightly different form, as the Lent Addresses in York Minster during Lent 2001. Chapter 7 first appeared, in a slightly different form, as a lecture in the 'Town and Gown' series of the College of York St John in March 2002, though it should be said that it first grew out of the discussions we had in our Lent House Groups in the Minster in 2001. I am grateful both to the Minster and to the College for the opportunities they gave me to do the original thinking and writing, though neither institution bears any responsibility for what I have done.

Jonathan Draper
York Minster

1

Setting the Scene

Christian discipleship – what it means to follow Christ – is about immersing ourselves in the life, words and works of Jesus in the context of prayer. Prayer is not simply or primarily about a form of words but, following the example of Jesus, is primarily a way of life; a way of orientating our wills to God's will. Prayer is much more than kneeling down in church from time to time – it requires a Christ-like openness to God, exploring our faith, growing into Christ and engaging with the world. It also requires change. Prayer, like theology for St Anselm, is about faith seeking understanding; trying to orientate our will to God's.

Faith seeking understanding is the most profound and most authentic kind of spirituality. If I may fly in the face of current thinking for a moment, spirituality is much more about attending to God than it is about getting in touch with yourself or feeling at one with the universe. Of course attending to God *will* bring us to the most important kinds of self-knowledge, and attending to God *will* make us feel at one with the universe, for we will be at one with God. But these are not an end in themselves: they are by-products of a much more profound process – the process of becoming Christ-like.

I'd like to dwell on this matter of spirituality a little. There are some – Christians among them – who think that the spiritual is something that is the opposite of the material. And on a not very profound level there is something in that. Material things and concerns can stand in the way of taking the values of God and of God's kingdom seriously. But on a more profound level there can be no such distinction. Our belief that God took on human flesh, the very material stuff out of which we and all things are made, in order to accomplish our spiritual liberation and to show us godly ways in action should enable us to see that, far from being a hindrance to our spirituality, material things and existence are actually the vehicle of our spirituality. There is no aspect of ourselves or our lives that stands outside the arena of God's concern or that, in itself, has nothing to do with the spiritual. God is to be found and met every bit as much through our bodily existence as through the most sublime of our thoughts and feelings. After all, the Word became flesh and in him we are able to see the glory of God.

So becoming Christ-like is a matter of taking a disciplined approach to every aspect of our lives, and this is what spirituality is. The first followers of Jesus were called his 'disciples' precisely because they accepted the disciplines of following him. They watched him deal lovingly with those in need; they watched him denounce hypocrisy and complacency; they watched him struggle with the full implications of his commitment to God; they drank in his every word and deed, becoming apprentices of the kingdom of God. And we are called to the same kind of discipleship, the same sort of apprenticeship. We too are called to sit at his feet as he brings us words of life; we too are called to understand and fight against the hypocrisy and complacency that lead people away from God (whether in the Church or the world); we too are called to commit ourselves to God in a way that just might change the world. This is the kind of spirituality that wells up from inside us as we allow the Spirit of God to open our hearts and minds and eyes to see God at work in our world. It is a spirituality that says that the world need not be the way it is, because God's love lived in us offers an alternative.

Spirituality, then, isn't just a matter of certain kinds of emotional or intellectual experiences or states. Being a spiritual person is really nothing more than being a godly person: it is to put your whole self at the disposal of God, to work with God in bringing in God's kingdom of righteousness, justice and peace.

Putting yourself at God's disposal is the fundamental attitude of the Christian. It is to say with Jesus in the Garden of Gethsemane, before the great and terrible climax of his ministry, 'Not my will, but your will be done.' The point of almost all that we do as Christians is to come to an understanding of what God's will is, and do it.

There is a little bit of a spiritual paradox here, which concerns how we come to know and understand anything about God or God's will. In part we can come to know something about God and God's will through what we might call the accumulated wisdom and experience of countless generations of Christians before us. We can learn from the Bible, from the witness of martyrs and saints, from the considered writings of the great theologians, pastors and mystics. We can learn from those around us in our own day, as millions try to live a Christ-like life in many and varied contexts. And, importantly, we can learn from each other.

That, however, is not the whole story. The paradox of spirituality and a godly life is that once you have determined to put yourself at God's disposal you learn most about God and God's will from the experience of trying to live a godly life. *Being* godly leads to an understanding of God and godliness. As the seminal seventeenth-century Anglican thinker Richard Hooker put it, 'Holiness precedes the knowledge of God.' There can be no separation of theory and practice in the Christian faith. It is not like a university department where you might have a theoretical science and an applied science; there is no such thing as 'theoretical godliness'. Knowing all there is to know about God without 'applied godliness' is empty, meaningless knowledge. The letter of James puts this well:

> Be doers of the word, and not merely hearers who deceive themselves. For if any are hearers of the word and not doers, they are like those who look at themselves in a mirror; for they look at themselves and, on going away, immediately forget what they were like. But those who look into the perfect law, the law of liberty, and persevere, being not hearers who forget but doers who act – they will be blessed in their doing.
>
> (James 1.23–25)

And a little later in the same letter he speaks specifically about having a theoretical knowledge of God when he writes,

> What good is it, my brothers and sisters, if you say you have faith but do not have works? . . . You believe that God is one; you do well. Even the demons believe – and shudder . . . For just as the body without the spirit is dead, so faith without works is also dead.
>
> (James 2.14, 19, 26)

The knowing and the doing belong inseparably together in an endless cycle, each informing and enriching the other.

I've entitled this chapter 'Setting the Scene' and we've begun to do that by trying to understand the basic approach to the Christian life. I now want to shift emphasis a little by looking more closely at the way in which Jesus set the scene for his ministry, and how that can help us set a pattern for our own discipleship.

In Luke's Gospel, chapter 4, we have the story of the beginning of Jesus' ministry.

Jesus, full of the Holy Spirit, returned from the Jordan and was led by the Spirit in the wilderness, where for forty days he was tempted by the devil. He ate nothing at all during those days, and when they were over, he was famished. The devil said to him, 'If you are the Son of God, command this stone to become a loaf of bread.' Jesus answered him, 'It is written, "One does not live by bread alone." '

Then the devil led him up and showed him in an instant all the kingdoms of the world. And the devil said to him, 'To you I will give their glory and all this authority; for it has been given over to me, and I give it to anyone I please. If you, then, will worship me, it will all be yours.' Jesus answered him, 'It is written, "Worship the Lord your God, and serve only him." '

Then the devil took him to Jerusalem, and placed him on the pinnacle of the temple, saying to him, 'If you are the Son of God, throw yourself down from here, for it is written, "He will command his angels concerning you, to protect you", and "On their hands they will bear you up, so that you will not dash your foot against a stone." '

Jesus answered him, 'It is said, "Do not put the Lord your God to the test." ' When the devil had finished every test, he departed from him until an opportune time.

Then Jesus, filled with the power of the Spirit, returned to Galilee, and a report about him spread through all the surrounding country. He began to teach in their synagogues and was praised by everyone.

When he came to Nazareth, where he had been brought up, he went to the synagogue on the sabbath day, as was his custom. He stood up to read, and the scroll of the prophet Isaiah was given to him. He unrolled the scroll and found the place where it was written:

'The Spirit of the Lord is upon me, because he has anointed me to bring good news to the poor. He has sent me to proclaim release to the captives and recovery of sight to the blind, to let the oppressed go free, to proclaim the year of the Lord's favour.'

And he rolled up the scroll, gave it back to the attendant, and sat down. The eyes of all in the synagogue were fixed on him. Then he began to say to them, 'Today this scripture has been fulfilled in your hearing.'

(Luke 4.1–21)

It is quite clear from the beginning of the story that Jesus followed a pattern of life similar to our own in getting to the point of putting himself at God's disposal. He grew up attending synagogue, no doubt picked up much from his reading of Scripture and listening to his parents and others. Now he was ready to make it all his own and to embark on a public ministry.

Before he does that we have the famous story of the temptation in the wilderness. Jesus is presented with a variety of worldly temptations and refuses them all, knowing that none of them are routes by which he can serve God. These are the same kinds of temptations we all face, and are all forms of the temptation to use our power to meet our own needs. Jesus refuses them all.

He then goes on to his home town of Nazareth and, on the Sabbath day, goes to the synagogue as was his custom. Whether Jesus usually did a reading and then sat down to teach, we can never know. But on this occasion he does both, and his public ministry is launched.

It is also interesting to note where Jesus launches his public ministry. He avoids the temptation of making a splash with a big publicity campaign centred on Jerusalem. Instead he begins in the poor, rural backwater of Nazareth – a place contemptuously dismissed by his sophisticated opponents at another time when they ask if anything good can come out of Nazareth. Jesus starts his ministry as he means to continue.

The passage he chose to read from Isaiah set his ministry in the opposite corner from the temptations he has just refused. He sees himself as anointed by God to use his power to serve the needs of others, especially those who are in greatest need. If his temptation was to use his power to serve his own needs, his ministry is focussed on the needs of others.

There are some who spiritualize this passage in a rather old-fashioned way. They see the poor as those who are poor in the things of God. They see the captives as those who are enslaved to material things or to ideas that keep them from God. They see the blind as those who are spiritually blind, unable to see the truth of God. They see the oppressed as those who are weighed down by the burdens and cares of life.

I'm sure that all of these things are true and that the year of the Lord's favour and the ministry of Jesus are for them too. But I think we must not forget the primary meaning of all this as well. The poor to whom Jesus directs his ministry are also those who are materially poor; the captives are those enslaved; the blind are those who cannot see; the oppressed are those who are ground down by social, economic and political forces. This is a context in which theoretical and applied godliness meet by intention and design, and a spirituality established that is meant to change the world.

This is where our discipleship starts as well. First in putting ourselves at God's disposal; second in refusing to see the point of our discipleship as serving our own needs; and third in committing ourselves to learning about God and God's will by serving the needs of others wherever we happen to be.

The scene is set for us now and we can see the beginnings of our discipleship. As we go on, we will learn more. We will see something of what it means to attend to God. We will see something of what is entailed in exploring our faith. We will see something of what it might mean to grow into Christ. We will see something of what it means to engage with the world, and how that can help us grow into Christ and will lead us to more exploration of our faith. And we will then see something of what it might mean to be the Body of Christ in the world.

2

Attending to God

If our Christian discipleship begins with putting ourselves at God's disposal, the most important thing we
can do to make that happen is to attend properly to
God. Attending to God is first of all an attitude and
only then a matter of what we do. The attitude is
simple but crucial and can be seen in the pattern of
Jesus' ministry. When you read through the Gospel of
Luke, for instance, the first third or so of the book is
made up of unconnected stories about Jesus going to
various places, and preaching or healing the sick or
casting out demons. In between the stories, often at the
end of one or the beginning of the next, the writer says
something like what we find in Luke 5.15–16:

> But now more than ever the word about Jesus
> spread abroad; many crowds would gather to
> hear him and to be cured of their diseases. But he
> would withdraw to deserted places and pray.

We find a similar remark in Luke 6.12: 'Now during
those days he went out to the mountain to pray; and he
spent the night in prayer to God.'

We see in these times of withdrawal a bit of a pattern in the ministry of Jesus, one he carried on even into the Garden of Gethsemane on the night he was betrayed. Times of high activity as he set about doing God's will followed by times of quiet reflection, times of attending to God. And this pattern of activity and reflection should form the basic pattern for our discipleship as well.

Attending to God, as I have mentioned already, is first of all an attitude. And, not to put too fine a point on it, I think it is an attitude that begins when we shut up and start to listen; listen to what God is telling us through whatever means that might be. Attending to God happens when we stop coming to God with our own agenda and pay attention to God's agenda. Attending to God happens when we stop trying to tell God things and listen with an open mind, as Jesus did, to the Spirit of God working in us.

It is remarkable how self-conscious, even self-centred our spirituality can be at times. We always seem to come to God with a bag full of concerns and a bucket full of our own needs and desires, and rarely come with empty bags and buckets seeking to have them filled. In part this is because we often fail to recognize the second central paradox of the Christian faith. In the last chapter we saw the paradoxical truth that we come to know something of God and God's will by trying to live godly lives. Now we see the paradox that the more we seek to fulfil our own needs through our spirituality the more unlikely we are to find them met. Or put the other way round, we will only find our true fulfilment by seeking the fulfilment of others. As Jesus puts it,

> If any want to become my followers, let them deny themselves and take up their cross daily and follow me. For those who want to save their life will lose it, and those who lose their life for my sake will save it.
>
> (Luke 9.23–24)

That was from Luke's Gospel, though the exact same saying is recorded in all the Gospels, and even appears twice in Luke. Matthew follows it with another paragraph, which makes it clear that losing your life for Christ's sake includes all the kinds of hospitality, care and service we show to others in Christ's name.

Spirituality as me looking for ways in which to be a more complete, whole or fulfilled person is one of the great fallacies of our age, and a fallacy that has taken people in all sorts of strange directions. That kind of self-focussed spirituality is the precise opposite of Christian spirituality, which is living a godly life for the sake of others. And therein lies the paradox. If you really do want self-fulfilment and wholeness as a person then don't try to find it. Lose yourself for

Christ's sake in seeking the fulfilment of others and you will have joy and life in all its fullness. The more you seek it for yourself the more it will elude you.

Genuine Christian spirituality and self-discipline is about how my focus on God leads me to focus on others. The prophet Isaiah records God as saying this to those who would be zealous in their devotion:

> Is not this the fast [the self-discipline] that I choose: to loose the bonds of injustice, to undo the thongs of the yoke, to let the oppressed go free, and to break every yoke? Is it not to share your bread with the hungry, and bring the home-less poor into your house; when you see the naked, to cover them, and not to hide yourself from your own kin?
>
> (Isaiah 58.6–7)

Godly spirituality is about embodying godly values in the real world in which we live; and not only far away, but here at home as well.

So attending to God is first of all an attitude of listening to God, of seeking to bring fulfilment and wholeness to others, and of losing yourself in the business of following Christ. Christian spirituality is about service.

Most Christians will be familiar with the story from Matthew's Gospel where the mother of James and John comes to Jesus on the quiet and begs a favour of him, that her sons might sit on his right and left hands in his kingdom. We need to remember the context of this story. Jesus was on his way to Jerusalem towards the end of his ministry, and he took the disciples aside on the way and said to them,

> See, we are going up to Jerusalem, and the Son of Man will be handed over to the chief priests and scribes, and they will condemn him to death; then they will hand him over to the Gentiles to be mocked and flogged and crucified; and on the third day he will be raised.
>
> (Matthew 20.18–19)

It is in this context that the mother of James and John approaches Jesus with her request.

The other disciples, when they heard about this, were pretty cross. Yet even with all their time with Jesus they did not always attend very closely to what he said and did. So Jesus speaks to them all and says,

> You know that the rulers of the Gentiles lord it over them, and their great ones are tyrants over them. It will not be so among you; but whoever wishes to be great among you must be your servant, and whoever wishes to be first among you must be your slave; just as the Son of Man

came not to be served but to serve, and to give his
life a ransom for many.

(Matthew 20.25–28)

'It will not be so among you.' It took the disciples a
long time finally to understand that following Jesus
was to be different. I guess the truth is that we all find it
hard to be as attentive to God as we should be, no
matter how much we try and no matter how close to
God we think we might be.

What, then, are the ways in which we can actually
be attentive? We need to begin with the notion of
listening to God, and there are many ways in which we
can do that.

First of all there are some obvious ways, and we
could do much worse than simply listening to God as
God speaks to us through the Bible. Reading the Bible
and letting it inform, challenge and shape our thinking
is a good way to listen to God. For in it we find God
speaking to us through God's people as they struggle
with exactly the same things with which we struggle;
namely, how to be the people of God in the world, how
to live by godly values in an ungodly world, how to live
together in such a way that we become ourselves a
witness to the truth of God.

But don't read the Bible as if it was a rule book, a
sort of religious equivalent to the *Highway Code*. Read
it instead with a view to picking out the principles by

which a godly life can be lived. Notice, for instance, how Jesus interacts with people. Look at the kind of faith that Jesus praises. See the purposes for which Jesus gives himself up to death for our sake. See the faithfulness and outrageous generosity with which God deals with God's people through the ages, and learn the kind of generosity God asks of us. Let the word of God come off the page and into your life.

But don't stop there. There are many other ways in which we can listen to God. Amazingly enough we may hear God speaking through each other, not only as individuals, but also as the Body of Christ. In worship, in study, in prayer, in the way we lead our lives, even in casual conversation, God may speak to us. But we will hear only if we are prepared to listen; we will hear only if we expect to hear.

God may speak to us through all sorts of things and people; after all, there is nothing in all creation that can separate us from the love of God. The other side of that is that *anything* in all creation may speak to us of the love of God, may be the means by which we learn something of what God's love might mean. We need to develop a spirituality with a genuinely catholic outlook.

By a catholic outlook I don't just mean the kind of spirituality usually associated with Catholic churches, though that too can be a means of listening to God. What I really mean is an attitude that is open to anything – everything – being the means by which God might speak to us, not just the usual things. We need to cultivate a willingness to be surprised by God.

I want to emphasize here the universality of the Christian vision. God is the God of the whole world and everything and everyone in it. God's concern is for all of the world and all of its people; no one and no thing stands outside that concern. Just as importantly the work of the Holy Spirit of God takes place in the whole world and not just in certain sanitized bits of it. To understand this is to look at the world in a different way. Of course we should expect to meet God and be able to listen to God when we gather for worship, or do our private devotions or Bible study. But we should also learn that we can expect to be encountered by God wherever we are, and whoever we are talking to. There are no God-free exclusion zones.

We will, however, have to learn to listen and how to hear in new ways if we are to attend to God outside our usual haunts. How do you learn to hear what God is saying in the aftermath of a natural disaster or a major accident? How do we hear what God is saying when we speak to a person of another faith?

There is a story that shows another way in which Jesus attends to God, and is precisely about an encounter with a person of another faith. The story is from Matthew 15.21–28.

Jesus left that place and went away to the district of Tyre and Sidon. Just then a Canaanite woman from that region came out and started shouting, 'Have mercy on me, Lord, Son of David; my daughter is tormented by a demon.' But he did not answer her at all. And his disciples came and urged him, saying, 'Send her away, for she keeps shouting after us.' He answered, 'I was sent only to the lost sheep of the house of Israel.' But she came and knelt before him, saying, 'Lord, help me.' He answered, 'It is not fair to take the children's food and throw it to the dogs.' She said, 'Yes, Lord, yet even the dogs eat the crumbs that fall from their masters' table.' Then Jesus answered her, 'Woman, great is your faith! Let it be done for you as you wish.' And her daughter was healed instantly.

In this story we see Jesus moving in his relationship to this woman from ignoring her, through being brutal to her, to praising her faith. She is a foreigner and of another religion (and worst of all, of course, a woman), and yet through this encounter Jesus is changed. And it happens not only because Jesus stops and thinks and prays from time to time, but also because he is also alert to the possibilities of God at all times. Attending to God is simply a part of his nature.

Whatever the circumstances, wherever we are and whoever we are engaged with, we can hear God speaking to us if we have put ourselves at God's disposal; if we are, as it were, tuned in. And we stay tuned in by focussing our attention on doing those things that God would have us do.

I think there is also a clue in another short story from Luke's Gospel:

> An argument arose among them [the disciples] as to which of them was the greatest. But Jesus, aware of their inner thoughts, took a little child and put it by his side, and said to them, 'Whoever welcomes this child in my name welcomes me, and whoever welcomes me welcomes the one who sent me; for the least among all of you is the greatest.'
>
> John answered, 'Master, we saw someone casting out demons in your name, and we tried to stop him, because he does not follow with us.' But Jesus said to him, 'Do not stop him; for whoever is not against you is for you.'
>
> (Luke 9.46–50)

Here we find the disciples once again trying to work out what greatness is in the kingdom of God. We also have the usual reply of Jesus that it is about service. But we also find the disciples complaining that someone who was not a part of their circle was casting out demons in Jesus' name. They don't like that, because that person isn't under their control and they try to stop him. Jesus tells them, in effect, not to be silly: whoever is not against you is for you.

Jesus is telling his disciples – and us – that we should be prepared to work with and acknowledge the godly work of others even if they are not of our group or under our control – whatever control that may be. We should expect to find allies in the work of the kingdom of God because the wind of the Spirit of God blows where it will and we have no control over it. Our job is to recognize God's work wherever and by whomever it is done. That is what it means to attend to God: to recognize the signs of godliness and learn from them; to be, like Jesus, alert to the possibilities of God.

3

Exploring our Faith

The beginnings of our discipleship are found in putting ourselves at God's disposal. We attend to God by learning to recognize the signs of godliness wherever we encounter them and by whomever they are done. We can also attend to God as we take the time to explore our faith and the potential riches of it.

There are two basic views we can take on exploring our faith. The first is that we can work on the assumption that our faith is a bit like York Minster or any other great and complicated building. Faith is essentially a completed structure about which we can always learn more, but which is also in its more or less finished form. The second is that we can work on the assumption that our faith is a bit like our understanding of the universe. We know enough to be getting on with, but also know that our knowledge is essentially incomplete, limited and partial.

I incline very much to the second of these views. Like a physicist whose experimental results create surprise and raise basic questions about what has gone before, I still find being a follower of Jesus has surprises for me, which sometimes do call into question what has gone before. Let me give you an example to illustrate what I mean.

Not long ago I was invited to preach near York at a service to mark the Week of Prayer for Christian Unity. I gladly accepted because I have always had an active interest in ecumenism.

The theme for that year's Week of Prayer for Christian Unity was 'Together on the Way': a typically anodyne kind of slogan. The subtitle was Jesus' famous line, 'I am the way, the truth and the life'. In the course of preparing the sermon, I spent some time looking again at the passage from John 14, where Jesus says this. Reading around this saying and looking at the wider context, an idea suddenly came to me; one that I'm sure has been blindingly obvious to everyone else, but which struck me very forcibly. In the passage Jesus makes clear, among other things, that the absolute foundation of his self-understanding and his ministry is his unity with God:

Whoever has seen me has seen the Father. How can you say, 'Show us the Father'? Do you not believe that I am in the Father and the Father is in me? The words that I say to you I do not speak on my own; but the Father who dwells in me does his works.

(John 14.9–10)

Jesus also makes it clear later in this passage that the basis of *our* discipleship is to be found in our unity with him and with each other. This is even clearer in Jesus' great prayer in the Garden of Gethsemane just before his betrayal and arrest.

> I ask not only on behalf of these, but also on behalf of those who will believe in me through their word, that they may all be one. As you, Father, are in me and I am in you, may they also be in us, so that the world may believe that you have sent me. The glory that you have given me I have given them, so that they may be one as we are one, I in them and you in me, that they may be completely one, so that the world may know that you have sent me and have loved them even as you have loved me. Father, I desire that those also, whom you have given me, may be with me where I am, to see my glory, which you have given me because you loved me before the foundation of the world.
>
> (John 17.20–24)

So far so good.

Then the idea came upon me. If our unity with Christ *and* with each other is the foundation of our faith, and if that is how the world will know God's love, then what does all this ecumenical stuff mean? The whole basis of the modern ecumenical movement has been the idea of a sort of pilgrimage towards unity. But we're not supposed to be on a pilgrimage to unity, we're supposed to be on a pilgrimage to God and the kingdom of God, and unity is where we begin. And if unity is where our discipleship begins, then we haven't got very far in our discipleship, let alone in our pilgrimage towards the kingdom of God. Even after 2,000 years we have hardly moved off the starting blocks in our discipleship, and it's not surprising that the world doesn't know or believe in God's love in the way we would hope.

This was as much of a surprise to me as was the discovery by astronomers not long ago that there is a black hole at the centre of our galaxy. It has begun the creation of a shift in my approach to the whole edifice of our faith. It has set me off on a voyage of exploration that is going to take some time.

Now it happens that I like surprises, though I realize that not everyone else does. It is, in some senses, much more comforting to view our faith as a relatively settled matter and that our discipleship is mostly a matter of understanding it better and gradually learning to make it our own. If, however, our knowledge of our faith and of our God is something that develops as we make the attempt to live godly lives, then we should not be surprised that our view of our faith changes as we go along. And if our understanding of our faith doesn't change in response to our experience of it, then I suspect our faith is not very alive. Or perhaps it might be that we lack the confidence to allow our faith to develop.

I suspect that this is more often the case than we care to admit. I blame it on the clergy. For most of the history of the Church the needs of lay people, in terms of equipping them for exploring their faith and making it truly their own, have been largely ignored. And worse, the riches that lay people have to contribute to the Church and its ministry have been largely, and patronizingly, rejected. We are now reaping that particular whirlwind. We have suddenly been awakened as out of sleep by a variety of crises and rediscovered our need of lay people in the Church. And not surprisingly many have asked why a historic reluctance to include lay people at the heart of the Church has suddenly turned into a desire to involve them at every level. Need has made us aware of what we should really have known all along: that the Church is the people of God, and that while some of those people have been chosen and authorized to carry out particular forms of ministry, the Church does not exist for and by them. We clergy have signally failed in an important part of our ordination charge, that of teaching and encouraging by word and example. And we are only beginning to explore what it might mean, in the words of the Anglican ordinal, to join with lay people in a common witness to the world. The rather patronizing attitude that 'Father knows best' is coming (slowly) to an end.

So the matter of exploring our faith is not a luxury to be taken up as and when clergy feel inclined to allow it to happen. It is now, I would like to argue, a matter of some urgency. So what might it mean to explore our faith? How do we go about it?

We need to begin where we begin our discipleship. We need to put ourselves at God's disposal, we need to set about living a godly life, and we need to take time to attend to God. But we need to do that together. I would like us to get away from the idea that Christianity is fundamentally about me and my relationship to God and my eternal destiny. Fundamentally, Christianity is about the mission of God in the world. And the mission of God in the world is to create a people who will work with God in bringing about the kingdom God seeks for all of creation. The whole of the Old Testament is about how a disparate band of people learn how to become the people of God. Much of the New Testament is taken up with exploring what it means to be the Body of Christ and how we are to be God's people in and for the world. So we need to start by rediscovering our need for each other and the processes of learning with and from each other. We need to start by learning what it means to be the Body of Christ as we join with God in God's mission in the world.

We also need to live our lives with our eyes open and learn to see the world as God sees it. Our exploration of our faith comes as we ask questions of ourselves and our experience. How can we serve the cause of godliness in any given context or relationship? In what way is what we are doing serving the causes of godliness and human flourishing? What can we learn from our experience that will bring us to a better understanding of God and godliness? We need to learn the skills of living godly lives and asking godly questions.

We also need to learn not to be afraid to ask questions or to express opinions. We need to realize that our churches (the Church itself) will not fall down if we think thoughts or express views that do not coincide with the received tradition. Jesus suggests that, as we give ourselves to the Spirit of God at work in us and in the world, the Spirit will also lead us deeper into truth. There is more for us to learn, more to discover about our faith, new directions in which our discipleship might take us as we put ourselves at God's disposal.

This is a delicate matter, however. We are a part of the people of God, and not the whole thing. And the community of the people of God in the world not only extends throughout the whole world, but through time as well. This means that we not only have much to learn from Christians living in other contexts and cultures, but also from Christians living in other times. The wisdom of the past is not to be discarded lightly; nor is it to be followed slavishly, for its own sake. Part of what it means to explore our faith is to keep an open dialogue going between ourselves and others in every place and time who also seek to follow Christ.

This is actually an exciting thing; it is also from time to time a sobering thing. Some years ago I was a participant in a World Council of Churches consultation at the Ecumenical Institute at Bossey in Switzerland. Among the other participants was a Korean theologian who spoke with some passion about how living the gospel could be a dangerous business. Teaching, as I was at the time, in a theological college and in one of our ancient universities, I didn't feel in any particular danger, except perhaps from boredom. During the course of the consultation, however, it emerged that this Korean theologian had been imprisoned and tortured by his government for his faith, for seeking to serve the needs of those who were most oppressed in his society. It was a humbling experience to realize the cost of this man's faith. It was also a learning experience. From him I gained a renewed sense of the importance of the gospel to the social and political needs of the world. My faith horizons were expanded.

It is also important to remind ourselves that exploring our faith is a lifelong activity. There is no point along the way in which we can say that we have arrived, no point at which we can relax and feel that we have done enough. So like attending to God, exploring our faith is also as much a matter of attitude as anything else. If attending to God is a matter of being constantly alert to the possibilities of God, exploring our faith is a matter of being constantly alive to the potential riches of our faith and not to settle for a less rich version of it.

There is also a spiritual aspect to this and a paradox. The paradox is pretty easy to state: the more we learn of God and what God demands of us the more we know how little we know. Exploring our faith is not like learning a fixed body of knowledge. Exploring our faith is about a developing relationship with a God who is alive and infinite, surpassing all that we can know, believe or do. It takes not only a lifetime of attentive learning, it takes an eternity. To explore our faith, to allow our faith to grow and develop and change is to open ourselves to the possibilities of God in a fundamental way, a way that just might challenge the foundations of who we are.

This is also the spiritual aspect. The spirituality of exploring our faith is to make ourselves the earthen vessels of which St Paul speaks, into which God wishes to pour the Holy Spirit to manifest God's power and love through us. The fundamental attitude of the spiritually alive is one of openness to God, an openness so complete that we can be filled by God's Spirit and empowered to live Christ's risen life in and for the world. The result of this openness and commitment is a serious responsibility. St Paul puts it like this:

From now on, therefore, we regard no one from a human point of view; even though we once knew Christ from a human point of view, we know him no longer in that way. So if anyone is in Christ, there is a new creation: everything old has passed away; see, everything has become new! All this is from God, who reconciled us to himself through Christ, and has given us the ministry of reconciliation; that is, in Christ God was reconciling the world to himself, not counting their trespasses against them, and entrusting the message of reconciliation to us. So we are ambassadors for Christ, since God is making his appeal through us; we entreat you on behalf of Christ, be reconciled to God. For our sake he made him to be sin who knew no sin, so that in him we might become the righteousness of God.

(2 Corinthians 5.16–21)

Read again the words St Paul uses to describe what it means to live the gospel and to describe our work as those reconciled to God in Christ. We are a new creation; we are ministers of reconciliation; we are ambassadors for Christ; we are to become the righteousness of God.

This is powerful and demanding stuff. To give ourselves to Christ is automatically to open ourselves to change and to the job of representing God to the world.

We are to become the righteousness of God. This means allowing ourselves to be remade by God into the image of Christ, to become Christ for the world, to become the voice and hands and very presence of Christ himself; to become his people.

Here we come, I think, to the heart of the Christian faith and to the heart of what Christian spirituality is. We have already seen that Christian spirituality is about the lives we live in God's name and about seeking the fulfilment of others. Now we see that it is also about growing into Christ to become the righteousness of God.

4

Growing into Christ

In this book we have so far seen three fundamental paradoxes of the Christian faith and Christian spirituality. First, that we *learn* about God's will by *doing* it; second, that we will only find self-fulfilment by seeking the fulfilment of others; and third, that the more we come to know God and what God demands of us the more we know how little we know. In looking at these paradoxical elements we've begun to see that our spirituality is about growing into Christ.

In examining what it means to grow into Christ I want to start with a substantial part of Ephesians.

I therefore, the prisoner in the Lord, beg you to lead a life worthy of the calling to which you have been called, with all humility and gentleness, with patience, bearing with one another in love, making every effort to maintain the unity of the Spirit in the bond of peace. There is one body and one Spirit, just as you were called to the one hope of your calling, one Lord, one faith, one baptism, one God and Father of all, who is above all and through all and in all.

But each of us was given grace according to the measure of Christ's gift. Therefore it is said, 'When he ascended on high he made captivity itself a captive; he gave gifts to his people.' (When it says, 'He ascended', what does it mean but that he had also descended into the lower parts of the earth? He who descended is the same one who ascended far above all the heavens, so that he might fill all things.) The gifts he gave were that some would be apostles, some prophets, some evangelists, some pastors and teachers, to equip the saints for the work of ministry, for building up the body of Christ, until all of us come to the unity of the faith and of the knowledge of the Son of God, to maturity, to the measure of the full stature of Christ. We must no longer be children, tossed to and fro and blown about by every wind of doctrine, by people's trickery, by their crafti-ness in deceitful scheming. But speaking the truth in love, we must grow up in every way into him who is the head, into Christ, from whom the whole body, joined and knitted together by every ligament with which it is equipped, as each part is working properly, promotes the body's growth in building itself up in love.

(Ephesians 4.1–16)

There is so much in the passage that it is difficult to know where to begin. I will start, however, with the twin goals of the passage, the second of which we will come back to in Chapter 6. The first is that we are to seek maturity, to grow into the full stature of Christ; and the second that together we are to become the fully functioning Body of Christ in the world.

As we have seen already, our discipleship is set within the context of our unity with Christ in the Spirit and with each other. For St Paul that is a sort of given. There is only one Lord, one faith, one baptism, one God and Father of all. Our unity is the basis of our life in Christ. And that is precisely the significance of the gifts of grace we are given by Christ. They are given to deepen our unity and enable us to function properly as the Body of Christ. From that basis we can grow into maturity, into the full stature of Christ.

Given that, we often remain remarkably childish about our faith. We get obsessed by trivial things: by doctrinal arguments, for example, when the real, grown-up business of the Christian faith is living the love of God for the world. We get obsessed by our own spiritual health, when the real, grown-up business of the Christian faith is to bring the health and healing of God's love to others. We even get obsessed by our own dignity and respectability as if they mattered in the kingdom of God, when the real, grown-up business of the Christian faith is the respect and dignity we accord to others. We remain stubbornly childish in our approach to our faith.

The problem with being childish in our approach to our faith is not primarily about your spiritual state or mine. Much more fundamentally the problem is about how being childish stymies the mission of God in the world. Every time we focus in on ourselves, every time we give in to the temptation to argue about how many angels can dance on the head of a microchip, every time we stand on our dignity, every time we let our agenda get in the way of God's agenda there is a small failure of mission. The world does not respond to the love of God as we would like because it does not see, in us, that it makes much difference. We are supposed to be a living sign of the possibilities that God holds out to the world, a community whose very existence stands as a witness that the world need not be the way it is. And yet we are perceived to be people whose religion brings about pettiness, hatred and injustice, and is irrelevant, rather than being seen as a body building itself up in love for service of the world.

That's why growing up into maturity, into the full stature of Christ is so important. So that through our unity, through the love we show for each other, through the service we offer the world with the same outrageous generosity God has shown to us, so that through all these things the world may believe, and believing, be transformed.

When I was in college in the United States, back in the dark ages of the early 1970s, I thought that the only way to be that kind of godly community in the world was to withdraw from the world into some form of Christian commune. Like the desert fathers of the early Church, I thought that if we could keep ourselves untainted by the world, and free from the temptations of the world, the flesh, and the devil, we could find our salvation and draw others in. We could create a kind of shelter from the storms of modern living, safe from the pernicious influences of secular ideas and the degeneration of society. I even had the long hair, beard and beads that went along with that kind of view.

The more I looked at the life of Jesus, however, and the more I saw how his times of withdrawal *from* the world were designed better to equip him for his ministry *in* the world, the more I grew disenchanted with the safe-haven view of Christianity. Jesus didn't hide away from anything. Instead he threw himself into the midst of the world, bringing the love of God and the gospel of reconciliation to all who would listen. He became one of us so that God's love and life might become an integral part of what it means to live a fully human life. This is what it means to grow into Christ: to give ourselves as fully and utterly to God's will and work as he did.

Like attending to God and exploring our faith, growing into Christ is fundamentally an attitude. And the attitude is described by a much abused word:

metanoia. *Metanoia* is the Greek word that is usually translated as 'conversion'. The way many Christians understand the word 'conversion' you would think it was the religious equivalent of changing your pounds for euros when you go on holiday: a significant, but not very life-changing exchange. In the vocabulary of my evangelical youth, conversion was the state of being changed from believing one set of – false – ideas to believing another set of – true – ideas. It was the equivalent of going to the religious *bureau de change* and changing your atheist, Buddhist, materialist or any other religious or intellectual currency for Christian currency.

Now I am deliberately caricaturing here. In my youth the point of conversion was for the person who did not know Christ to come to know him and be transformed by him. But the word *metanoia* is a much richer word than that. Of course it is about changing your mind, but it is also about repentance and a change of heart. Perhaps more importantly it is also about turning to face in another direction, about allowing your whole orientation to be changed. It is a fundamental shift of attitude and direction; from being and doing one kind of thing, to turn about and to do and be another.

Metanoia is the beginning of growing into Christ. It is as if we are walking in one direction and hear the words of Christ – 'Follow me' – and turn around to follow him in another direction. It is not just a turning-around; we also turn our backs on what went before. Following Christ is not a sort of 'add-on' to your life, like vitamins added to an otherwise useless breakfast cereal. Saying 'yes' to Christ is to say 'no' to many other things. By that I do not mean the traditional list of petty dos and don'ts usually associated with religious people. By saying 'yes' to Christ you are also saying 'yes' to life and all that makes life worth living. The 'no' you say is to all that stands in the way of life, that stands in the way of human flourishing. To say 'yes' to Christ is to make a truly positive and seriously challenging decision.

That decision is only the beginning of the adventure. As we try to live godly lives in and for the world, so we begin to discover the riches life can hold for those who follow after God. We begin to see the grandeur of God's vision for the world and the potential it holds out for all people. As we try to be the Body of Christ in the world, so we also begin to see the distance we have to go to grow into the full stature of Christ.

Growing into Christ is not unlike the business of growing into an adult. Indeed, St Paul uses this analogy:

And so, brothers and sisters, I could not speak to you as spiritual people, but rather as people of the flesh, as infants in Christ. I fed you with milk, not solid food, for you were not ready for solid food. Even now you are still not ready, for you are still of the flesh. For as long as there is jealousy and quarrelling among you, are you not of the flesh, and behaving according to human inclinations?

(1 Corinthians 3.1–3)

Infantile behaviour – behaviour that leads away from the unity essential to our discipleship, to our mission and to growing into the full stature of Christ – is to live according to the flesh and not according to the mind of Christ.

And these same ideas are echoed in Peter's first letter:

Rid yourselves, therefore, of all malice, and all guile, insincerity, envy, and all slander. Like newborn infants, long for the pure, spiritual milk, so that by it you may grow into salvation – if indeed you have tasted that the Lord is good.

Come to him, a living stone, though rejected by mortals yet chosen and precious in God's sight, and like living stones, let yourselves be built into a spiritual house, to be a holy priesthood, to offer spiritual sacrifices acceptable to God through Jesus Christ . . .

You are a chosen race, a royal priesthood, a holy nation, God's own people, in order that you

may proclaim the mighty acts of him who called
you out of darkness into his marvelous light . . .
Conduct yourselves honourably among the
Gentiles, so that, though they malign you as evil-
doers, they may see your honourable deeds and
glorify God when he comes to judge.

(1 Peter 2.1–5, 9, 12)

In both these passages we see the importance of
growing up, of putting behind us the childish ways that
block the mission of God in the world. The way we are
together as the Body of Christ, as God's own people, is
the measure of our spiritual maturity. If we want a
doubting world to believe that we – as the Body of
Christ – have something of value to offer them, then we
need to leave behind the pettiness of our childish ways
and seek the maturity of Christ himself.

There is one other passage in which St Paul uses the
image of childhood and adulthood to get his readers to
grow up into Christ, which I am somewhat reluctant to
use. It is, of course, 1 Corinthians 13, one of the most
abused passages in the Bible. It is St Paul's famous
'hymn to love', as some of the commentators have
called it, which begins 'If I speak in the tongues of
mortals and of angels, but do not have love, I am a
noisy gong or a clanging cymbal'. And the number of
dewy-eyed brides that have made me read it at
weddings has almost rendered it unusable for me. It is

not, of course, about the nature of the romantic love that wives and husbands ought to have for each other. It is not about romantic love at all. It is a description of the kind of love that should characterize the relations between Christians who have begun to become Christ-like. The greatest of the spiritual gifts for building up the body of Christ is the Christ-like love that never ends. Everything else may pass away, but love never ends. And it is in this context that St Paul urges his readers in Corinth to grow up.

> Love never ends. But as for prophecies, they will come to an end; as for tongues, they will cease; as for knowledge, it will come to an end. For we know only in part, and we prophesy only in part; but when the complete comes, the partial will come to an end. When I was a child, I spoke like a child, I thought like a child, I reasoned like a child; when I became an adult, I put an end to childish ways. For now we see in a mirror, dimly, but then we will see face to face. Now I know only in part; then I will know fully, even as I have been fully known. And now faith, hope, and love abide, these three; and the greatest of these is love.
>
> (1 Corinthians 13.8–13)

There are two really significant things in this passage. The first is that learning to love in Christ-like lives is what Christian or spiritual maturity is. The second is the grown-up recognition that no matter how Christ-like we become, no matter how mature, no matter how loving, we still, as it were, see through a glass darkly, as the old version puts it. But when all else is shown to be ephemeral, no matter how important and no matter how cherished, still faith, hope and love remain as the central planks of our discipleship. Faith in the Christ of God as the way to live our lives, as the truth of God, and as the life of the world; hope as unshakable trust in the possibilities of God; and love as the acted life of Christ in the world and among ourselves. Growing into Christ is to be liberated from pettiness and released for joyful service of Christ in the world on the basis of love; it is to become the righteousness of God.

5

Engaging with the World

So far in this book everything we have seen about spirituality and the Christian faith has led us to recognize the need we all have to grow into Christ, to become Christ-like in our loving service of one another and the world. One way or another 'the world' has been a theme running through it. It is *to* the world that Christ came; it was *for* the world that he lived and died; it was *in* the world that Christ proclaimed the kingdom of God; and it is *to* the world that we are sent as his people and in his name. As St John puts it early in his Gospel,

> God so loved the world that he gave his only Son, so that everyone who believes in him may not perish but may have eternal life. Indeed, God did not send the Son into the world to condemn the world, but in order that the world might be saved through him.
>
> (John 3.16–17)

'God so loved the world': these are the key words for the Christian faith, for Christian spirituality and for Christian mission.

In the last chapter I wrote that I had grown disenchanted with the safe-haven view of Christianity, where Christian spirituality is seen as withdrawing from the world into the Christian *laager* in order to remain untainted by the world. I have suggested throughout this book that real, grown-up Christian spirituality is about the lives we live in God's name in the world. This chapter, on engaging with the world, is about how we do that. 'God so loved the world' is about why.

Engaging with the world has a wide variety of aspects to it. Because Christian mission always takes place in a context, there will always be different ways in which engagement with the world takes place. What may be most important in one place and time may seem inappropriate in another. So to pretend that there are only certain kinds of ways in which Christians should engage with the world is to misunderstand the mission of God and to misunderstand the inner dynamic of the Christian faith with its need to be ever alert to the possibilities of God in every kind of context.

Given the intellectual climate of our time and society, with its pick-and-mix attitude to spirituality, ethics and structures of belief and action, there is a pressing need for us to engage with the world intellectually. We need to argue the Christian case in the marketplace of ideas. We need to seek to convince people that the Christian faith is credible, coherent with their experience and a viable way of living. None of that will be given automatic credence. We can no longer expect people to have much knowledge of the Christian faith, nor can we expect what knowledge they do have to be anything like accurate. So part of what it means to engage with the world in our generation is the old-fashioned-sounding business of apologetics: making the Christian case in language, ideas and, increasingly, images that people outside the community of faith can understand. We should not underestimate the size of this task.

This was brought home quite starkly to me when I was in a jewellers shop looking at earrings as a possible birthday present for my wife. While I was examining the range in one case, a young woman, probably 16 or 17, was talking to an assistant about the crosses in another case. It was a time when crosses were fashionable. As she looked at them she decided that she would like to see, as she put it, 'one with the little man on it'. She didn't have a clue what she was looking at. More than that, the central symbol of the Christian faith meant nothing at all to her. We have a huge job of communication to do if we are to recover anything of the meaning of the Christian faith and its symbols for this generation. So engaging with the world in part means making the Christian case in ways that people can understand. Like Jesus speaking in parables, picking up the everyday concerns and contexts of the people he addressed, we need to recover the ability to speak to people where they are and in a language that includes rather than excludes them.[1]

Engaging with the world, however, is not just a matter of saying or explaining things; it is also about being a part of things. We need, for instance, to engage with the world culturally. At various points in the history of the British Isles it could be said that the cultural life of the nation was a structure built on the Christian faith. Music, art, literature, even public holidays were permeated with the language, imagery and themes of the Christian faith. The central rites of passage in the lives of most people – births, marriages, and deaths – were celebrated or marked by Christian services. The Christian faith touched every aspect of life. This is no longer the case.

That is not to say that it should be the case, however, in the same kind of way. We no longer live in a society where the Christian faith has a respected voice or even an automatic place in the cultural life of the country. Ours is a multicultural, multi-ethnic and multifaceted society in which cultural contributions come from all sorts of different directions. And however complicated that might make life, it is essentially a good thing. We stand to be enriched by the variety of perspectives this brings, and the different views of the world – God's world – it allows us to see.

Because the Christian voice and perspective no longer have a controlling or even an automatic voice in our cultural life, we need to find new ways in which to engage with it and make our distinctive contribution. And we need to begin by being positive. Too often contemporary Christian contributions to culture seem only to take the form of complaints that our cultural life is simply going down the tubes. Carping from the sidelines will not win friends and influence people; it will only make them deaf to the legitimate range of contributions we would like to make. It is also to forget that God sent his Son into the world not to condemn it but to save and serve it.

We also need to recognize and celebrate the work of the Spirit of God in some of the contributions others who are not Christians have to make to our national cultural life. The unity that is the foundation of our own discipleship is also meant to be a model for the unity of all people in the kingdom of God. And unity in Christian terms is never uniformity; it is a unity of purpose expressed through a diversity of gifts, perspectives and contexts in which each can make their distinctive contribution to the kingdom God wishes for all the world. So in part, engaging with the world means playing a full, positive and open part in the cultural life of the nation.

Engaging with the world will also mean that we need to make our contribution to the moral and ethical debates of our time. This can be a difficult area since Christians do not speak with only one voice or from one perspective on moral issues. For perfectly respectable reasons, Christians sometimes find themselves on opposite sides of a given debate. But whatever our contribution it needs to be made as an offering and not as an attempt to control the debate. It also needs to be done with the greater principles of God's mission in the world in mind. We have said 'yes' to Christ and to all that makes for life, and 'no' to all that stands in the way of life or stands in the way of human flourishing.

That is not, of course, as simple as it sounds. Saying 'yes' to life may mean different things to different people and will almost certainly lead to pressures pulling the Christian in seemingly opposing directions. The question of abortion is one such issue. Even when the debate about abortion is stripped of all its trivial elements, there may still be different ways to answer 'yes' to life in that debate. It will not always be straightforward; and I think we need to resist the temptation to simplify the debate, as if one answer will always be right in all circumstances. As Lord Habgood once said in a debate in the Church of England's General Synod, 'For every difficult and complicated question there is an answer that is simple, easily understood – and wrong.' Love is a creative and dynamic principle, which will be expressed in different ways at different times and is not susceptible to legislation.

This is also an area that highlights the need for us to remember that engaging with the world is a process in which we take the risk of being changed by the encounter. Christians do not have a monopoly of moral and ethical insight, even if we do have distinctive points of view. Nevertheless we must be engaged, or we run the even greater risk of being marginalized in some of the most profound debates of our times.

More controversially, engaging with the world is also about the active participation of Christians in political and economic debates. I say 'more controversially' not because I think there is anything controversial about Christian involvement in politics, but because at least some others seem to think there is. Every time a church leader dares to make a contribution to a national debate they are told not to meddle in politics. The implication is that faith is only a personal and private matter and has nothing to do with society or the great issues of the day. The murdered Archbishop of El Salvador, Oscar Romero, put it very well when he said that when he gives bread to the poor they call him a saint; when he asks why the poor have no bread they call him a communist. When an Archbishop of Canterbury insists that the Argentinean as well as British dead should be prayed for at the end of the Falklands war, there is xenophobic uproar and he is accused of being 'political', as if prayer for the dead of an enemy country was being political and somehow in opposition to being faithfully Christian.

To suggest that the Christian faith is only a personal and private matter is a serious misrepresentation of the

Christian faith, but a popular one. We have already seen in previous chapters that the concern of God is for everyone and everything in creation, and that nothing stands outside the scope of God's concern for the world. For the Christian, God's concern is our concern, God's agenda is our agenda. There is nothing in all creation that stands outside God's vision for God's world. So the Christian faith has a contribution to make, no matter how unwelcome it might be.

This can be seen in looking at one of the great themes of the Old Testament: justice. The word 'justice' is used in basically three ways in the Old Testament. First, theologically, justice is used to describe the essential perfection of God both in Godself and in God's dealings with creation. Second, justice is a political virtue, which is to give every person their due. Third, justice is used to describe the way in which all people should deal with and relate to each other.

So justice is both a political and a religious theme. And to say 'yes' to justice is to say 'no' to injustice. It *is* to ask why the poor have no food, it is to pray for all who have died, it is to call governments, industries, armies, banks and individuals to account for their actions in terms of God's high standards of justice. We are called to echo the words of the psalmist:

God has taken his place in the divine council;
    in the midst of the gods he holds judgement:

'How long will you judge unjustly
   and show partiality to the wicked?
Give justice to the weak and the orphan;
   maintain the right of the lowly and the destitute.
Rescue the weak and the needy;
   deliver them from the hand of the wicked.'

(Psalm 82.1–4)

It is not insignificant that two of the issues over which
the churches have spoken with the most coherence in
the past 20 years, and for which they have been most
criticized for being political, have been over the state
of British inner cities and the issue of Third World
debt: that is, concerning the weak, the needy and the
destitute. The psalmist would see both of these as
straightforward issues of justice over which God's
people should, in God's name, have a concern, no
matter how hotly they are contested as political and
economic issues.

   Another, even more controversial, aspect of justice is
seen in Psalm 82 as well, and that is, to use the title of
David Sheppard's book, a *Bias to the Poor*.[2] Look at the
words that are used to say what should be done: 'give',
'maintain', 'rescue', 'deliver'. These are active words
requiring both action and attitude. And look at the
groups that are singled out: 'the weak', 'the orphan',
'the lowly', 'the destitute', 'the needy'. These are people
who have no economic or political status in society, and

yet are the object of God's special concern, and should be the object of our special concern as well. And you had better believe that engaging with these groups in a way that respects and empowers them in God's name will be unwelcome by those whose interests are served by ignoring them. I'm not quite sure why some Christians find offence with this idea. After all, Jesus made it perfectly plain at different times and in different ways in his ministry that the normal priorities of the world are to be overturned in the kingdom of God. But active Christian engagement with the world in the political and economic arenas, while it may give rise to controversy, is essential, but will not be cost-free. Indeed, the costs of engagement can be quite high, and not only in foreign places, but also here at home as well.

One of our great friends, who happens to be a woman priest and one of my son's godparents, was vicar of one of the most deprived of our inner-city estates. She went there because no man was willing to. One of the most significant social and economic issues affecting the estate was organized loan sharks; criminals lending poor people money at punitive rates of interest backed up by violence. In order to help rid the estate of this blight, she helped set up a credit union to assist people financially and at the same time help put the loan sharks out of business. It became successful enough that she was beaten up on her doorstep by one of the gangs who control the loan sharks. She paid a serious price for engaging with the world in God's name. But she also knew the fundamental truth that doing nothing is to collude with injustice. It is a failure of justice.

To live the gospel by engaging with the world is about putting our money where our mouth is; it's about putting flesh on the bones of our faith; it's about putting our faith – and our God – to the test of real, not virtual, discipleship. Perhaps most importantly of all, it is to give truth to our faith and to the depth of our spirituality. Engaging with the world means that we have begun to grow into Christ, and begun to learn what it means to attend to God and to explore our faith in a hands-on sort of way. It is to learn the difference between the observance of a religion and the living of a faith.

No one has put this point better than the prophet Micah:

> With what shall I come before the LORD,
>   and bow myself before God on high?
> Shall I come before him with burnt-offerings,
>   with calves a year old?
> Will the LORD be pleased with thousands of rams,
>   with tens of thousands of rivers of oil?
> Shall I give my firstborn for my transgression,
>   the fruit of my body for the sin of my soul?
> He has told you, O mortal, what is good;
>   and what does the LORD require of you

but to do justice, and to love kindness,
and to walk humbly with your God?
(Micah 6.6–8)

God is not impressed with our religious observance, no matter how rigorous or extreme. What God demands of us is that we should live our faith in a Christ-like and loving engagement with the world.

6

Being the Body of Christ in the World

In this chapter I want to begin to bring all the main themes of this book together by looking at what it might mean to be the Body of Christ in the world. I'd like to start, however, by taking a small step back to set something of the conceptual context not only for understanding what it might mean to be the Body of Christ, but also for all our talk about God. I think it is helpful if we understand something about the nature of the language we use about God and how that can be both a help and a hindrance.

It could be argued that this should have happened right at the beginning when we were setting the scene, and I wouldn't disagree with that. The reason for bringing it in now, however, is that we have come to a point where being really clear about the nature of the language we use about God is important.

The history of Christian spirituality and of thinking about the Christian faith is littered with fundamentalisms. A way of understanding the Christian faith is elevated to *the* way; a way of approaching Christian ethics is elevated to *the* way; a way of approaching God in worship and prayer is elevated to *the* way; *a* way of interpreting the Bible is elevated to *the* way. And so on. And most of these fundament-alisms focus on language. So as we come to the point of looking at a way of understanding what it means to be the Church by looking at what it might mean to be the Body of Christ, I would also like us to be clear about the language we are using.

All of the language we use about God is metaphori-cal; none of it is literally true. Now before you get too excited by that, I'd like you to stop and think about it for a moment. One of the fundamental insights of the Christian faith, attested to by all the saints, is that God is beyond our knowing, and in order to say anything about God we stretch our language to its limits and beyond. We speak about God – who is not the same kind of being we are – using language that can only describe who *we* are and what we know. And in order to make it clear that we are trying to talk about some-thing that is greater than we are, we make our language absolute.

For example, we understand something about power and might; we have experience of powerful people, or the might of events like earthquakes, wind and fire, the mightiest things we know. What we want to say is that God is mightier than all that, so we begin many of our prayers by saying 'Almighty God . . .' We are trying to describe our understanding and experience of God by applying earthly categories in their ultimate degree. We want to say that God knows us in a way we can never even know ourselves, so we call God 'all-knowing' or 'omniscient'; we want to say that God is beyond our understanding of space and time, so we call God 'ever-lasting' or 'eternal'. And so on. God is none of these things; except we have no other language and experience out of which to speak of God than our own. God is *not* like us, only bigger and better. God is God, and we are a part of God's creation; we are not God.

So the language we use is, to start with, inadequate to the task we ask of it. St Thomas Aquinas was so aware of the inadequacies of our language to say any-thing true about God, that he described our talk about God as taking the *via negativa*, the negative way. God is not weak as we are, so we talk about God's 'omni-potence'; God is not ignorant as we are, so we talk of God's 'omniscience'; God is not limited to one place and time as we are, so we talk of God's 'omnipresence', and so on. In saying these things we are not in fact describing God at all, except to say that God is not like us. But in this way we at least acknowledge both our limitations as human beings, and that God is God and not limited as we are.[1]

The question then arises about the truth of our language, and hence our understandings, about God. As I have already indicated, none of our language about God is literally true, but I don't think that means that our language and ideas about God are neces~~~ily untrue. With Janet Martin Soskice,[2] and others, I would like to argue that our language about God is – or can be – metaphorically true and can genuinely depict reality.

To say that is to say something about the nature of language and not necessarily to make a judgement about truth. Some things are literally true: to say I typed the draft of this book on my computer is to say something that is literally true, even if it's not very profound. To say that God is our rock may well be to say something true and profound, but it is not literally true. So to say that something is metaphorically true is to comment on the way in which truth is expressed – literally or metaphorically – and not to comment on the truth of what is expressed in that way.

Let me give you one more example. To say that Jesus is the 'lamb of God' is to say something of very great importance and deep truth for our understanding of Jesus and his death. But it is not literally true; Jesus was no more a lamb than I am an elephant. Though using the analogy of an elephant to depict something of the reality about me – size or speed, for instance – may be a way of speaking the truth.

Martin Luther was also very concerned about these matters and decided that the only truth we can speak about God is the truth about God found in Jesus. So through Jesus we find out something of God's compassion, righteousness, love and will, but that is all we can know. Anything outside the revelation of God in Jesus, as he saw it, is mere speculation and not really worth the time it takes. In fact Luther was clear that anything pretending to be knowledge of God outside Jesus was actually of the devil and positively evil.

While I may not want to go the whole way with Luther, he reminds us that for Christians, as Michael Ramsey put it, God is Jesus Christ-like.[3] We accept that through Jesus we can genuinely know something of God and speak of God in ways that are true, even if they are not literally true, and even if that is not the whole truth. Luther, again, was clear that when we see God through Jesus Christ we see God only as revealed to us and not as God is in Godself.

You may be wondering by now just what any of this has to do with Christian spirituality or faith. Apart from alerting us to the ever-present dangers of language-based fundamentalisms of any kind, I hope we will also be able to find this recognition that our language is limited to be a kind of liberation. To recognize, for example, that while calling God 'father' may well express an important truth to us, the recognition that it is not literally true can also liberate us from the tyranny of a single kind of language. It can allow us to find truth in other ways of depicting God through, say, other human relationships. Calling God 'mother', for instance, may express a different sort of truth to us, which 'father' simply cannot convey. Neither is literally true, but both can speak truth to us about our God.

To find liberation in a wide variety of images is not, of course, something new; only something we seem not to like very much. All of the great saints of the Christian faith have recognized the limitations of language and cast around for new ways of trying to convey their experience. But nowhere is this freedom found better used than in the Bible itself where God is depicted in almost every conceivable kind of way from king and father to chicken, she-bear and lover. Like our forebears in the faith, we need to rediscover our imagination as a tool for Christian spirituality and for exploring the Christian faith. We need to be alert enough to the possibilities of God to feel free to abandon one set of images or language when they obviously don't work and find another. We also need, of course, to recognize that this can be gain as well as loss. We stand to be enriched by getting off our mental tramlines and allowing the Spirit of God to enliven our minds.

We are a long way into this chapter and I am conscious that I have hardly mentioned the Body of Christ at all. But I hope you have begun to see how some of the strands that we have been looking at in the previous chapters are beginning to come together through this discussion of how we speak of God. A part of what this book has been about has been the attempt to get us to look at Christian spirituality and the Christian faith from a slightly different perspective so that as we come to look at what it might mean to be the Body of Christ we are prepared for the most important aspect of it. And that is that the Body of Christ is meant to be a living organism and not a corpse.

I take it that a core Christian belief is that Jesus – the head of the body – is alive, and that the God he called 'Father' is a living God, and that our faith is to be a living faith as well. For human beings, to live is to change, and I take it that being the Body of Christ in the world – because it implies growing into Christ the head – means to change a lot. At the very least it must mean, to keep with the analogy, growing up from infancy to adulthood, from childishness to maturity, from individualism to organism. Change is a subject to which I will return at greater length in Chapter 7.

The unity we have seen already as fundamental to our discipleship also forms the basis for St Paul's use of the body imagery. The classic text on the Church as the Body of Christ comes from 1 Corinthians.

> Just as the body is one and has many members, and all the members of the body, though many, are one body, so it is with Christ. For in the one Spirit we were all baptized into one body – Jews or Greeks, slaves or free – and we were all made to drink of one Spirit.
>
> Indeed, the body does not consist of one member but of many. If the foot were to say, 'Because I am not a hand, I do not belong to the body', that would not make it any less a part of the

body. And if the ear were to say, 'Because I am not an eye, I do not belong to the body', that would not make it any less a part of the body. If the whole body were an eye, where would the hearing be? If the whole body were hearing, where would the sense of smell be? But as it is, God has arranged the members in the body, each one of them, as he chose. If all were a single member, where would the body be? As it is, there are many members, yet one body. The eye cannot say to the hand, 'I have no need of you', nor again the head to the feet, 'I have no need of you.' On the contrary, the members of the body that seem to be weaker are indispensable, and those members of the body that we think less honourable we clothe with greater honour, and our less respectable members are treated with greater respect; whereas our more respectable members do not need this. But God has so arranged the body, giving the greater honour to the inferior member, that there may be no dissension within the body, but the members may have the same care for one another. If one member suffers, all suffer together with it; if one member is honoured, all rejoice together with it.

Now you are the body of Christ and individually members of it.

(1 Corinthians 12.12–27)

The great bulk of this passage is simply St Paul's slightly odd description, for his own purposes, of how he understands a body to work. A properly functioning body takes seriously all its many parts, and needs them all, no matter how lowly we think they are.

Look again, however, at the marvellous second sentence of this passage: 'For in the one Spirit we were all baptized into one body – Jews or Greeks, slaves or free – and we were all made to drink of one Spirit.' Here we have expressed not only the fundamental unity that stands at the heart of our spirituality and faith, but the essential equality of us all in the Spirit of Christ. All those things that normally divide us from each other no longer matter in the kingdom of God: religion or economic and political status mean nothing, for our unity in the Spirit overrides them all. And we only need to look at St Paul's letter to the Galatians to see that divisions between us based on race and gender don't matter either, for we are all members of one another in the Body of Christ.

As many of you as were baptized into Christ have clothed yourselves with Christ. There is no longer Jew or Greek, there is no longer slave or free, there is no longer male and female; for all of you are one in Christ Jesus.

(Galatians 3.27–28)

We really do need to learn to live this if we are to have any pretensions to being the Body of Christ. For being the Body of Christ is how we are called to be the Church, how we are to be Christ for the world, how we are to participate in the mission of God. And that is what the Church is for: to be Christ for the world, a model of the new creation, a living witness to the love and purposes of God. This is the heart of Christian spirituality, the heart of the Christian faith and the point of our existence. All we have to do now is live it.

Being the Body of Christ in the world is a process; in classic terms it is a process of action and reflection. The action of trying to live godly lives, and the reflection that leads us on in new and creative ways of being the Church for the world. There is, I'm afraid, no resting point, no settled place where we can set up camp and feel we have arrived. The only places where Christians have set up camp have the unacceptable names of 'complacency', 'fundamentalism' and 'head in the sand'. As we have seen already, to be human is to change; and to be a follower of Christ is to change often.

Our deepest spiritual needs are met in doing the will of God; that is, in being the Body of Christ in and for the world. We can only be the Body of Christ if we take seriously God's mission in the world, which is to create, ultimately, godly human community for the whole world. Our role in that is to put ourselves at God's disposal, to attend to God, to explore the ways in which we can be God's people, to grow into Christ and engage with the world. We are not the architects of the kingdom of God; we are the workforce. And the foundation of our spirituality, our discipleship and for being the Body of Christ in the world is, as we have seen in this book, our unity in Christ and with each other.

7

Change in Perspective

One of the themes running through this book in a relatively unexplored way is change. Coming to terms with change, especially for Christians, is so important that I want to end this book with an extended discussion of it. But a word of warning: this chapter will be more controversial and demanding than the others, for it touches on issues that matter greatly.

One of the reasons for writing this chapter about change (and I am sorry for being slightly parochial at this point, but I think it also applies to other churches) is that the institution for which I work – the Church of England – is, like many other institutions, going through a period of rapid and painful change. Nobody seems to like it, even though everyone pretends to think that change must happen. It is one of the delicious ironies of the Church of England that the more one talks about change the less likely it is to happen. When the evangelicals start to talk about the need for change, the traditionalists also suddenly feel the need to talk about the need for change. The more both of these groups talk about the need for change, the more liberal Anglicans also feel the need to get on the bandwagon. Every church will be able to identify groups or individuals who match this Anglican model. So everyone talks about the need for change, knowing that no two people you talk to mean the same thing by it and that, therefore, no change will ever take place. So perhaps when church leaders talk about the need for change it may be the same sort of use of language as when a Prime Minister says that one of his troubled ministers has his 'full backing'. We enter the 'Alice in Wonderland' world of language where words mean whatever you want them to mean.

The context for thinking about change, however, is infinitely worse in the Church than it is elsewhere. By that I do not mean that the Church is changing more than other institutions at a greater pace; just talk to the teachers to find out what rapid and constant change means. Nor do I mean that the Church necessarily has more changing to do than other institutions; we only have to look at some of our political institutions to see candidates for enormous change. The context for thinking about change in the Church is worse than elsewhere for two reasons. First, people think of God as unchanging and that, therefore, the truth about God and the ways in which that truth is expressed should also be unchanging. (This is a subject to which we will return.) And second, because of all the other changes taking place in our social, political, economic and personal lives, there needs to be something that doesn't change, some oasis of stability in which all of the other changes can be ignored and where things are 'the way they used to be', and the prime candidate for this oasis of retro-ignorance is the Church.

There is also a psychological reason why church people so often find it hard to contemplate change, and that is because of the association of change with death and decay. The hymn 'Abide with me' – itself a part of the seemingly unchanging repertoire of church hymns – can help us here. The second verse sums up neatly why so many church people find change alarming and difficult to do:

> Swift to its close ebbs out life's little day;
> Earth's joys grow dim, its glories pass away;
> Change and decay in all around I see:
> O thou who changest not, abide with me.

'Change and decay in all around I see'; no wonder church people find change so difficult.

I find this all a bit unreal. The real question that church people should be asking themselves is: Why do they expect things to stay the same? And I don't mean here just the outward form of church things. Even the church person most adamantly against change might be forced to admit that there is a case for stating eternal and unchanging truths in a different way in the twenty-first century than was the case in the first or fourth century – though even that is too much for some. What I really mean is real change in the substance of things such as doctrine and ethics and praxis. It's not clear to me why we should expect these to stay the same when human thinking has moved on. I'll use a controversial example to show what I mean.

Why should we expect our understanding of what it means for Jesus to be fully human not to have changed since the fourth century, when orthodox beliefs about the humanity of Jesus were laid down? The Church has liked to believe that Jesus was in every way human as we are. The Church could hold to that belief on the basis of fourth-century biology and still believe that Jesus had a human mother and a divine father. After all, in fourth-century biology, a woman was a mere receptacle for the fully formed human being supplied by the man. Twenty-first-century biology, let alone twentieth-century biology, of course, has shown us that a human being is a unique combination of the genetic material of the mother and the father, and that both are essential to making a real human person. More than that, twenty-first-century biology has shown us that the default position for the human person is female and that the male is a mutation of that. If this kind of information and understanding doesn't force substantial change on the theology of the Church, then church people should not be surprised that twenty-first-century people pay them and their ideas no attention whatsoever. So the real question is not why things change, but: Why do we expect things to stay the same? Taking on this challenge is a part of what it means to attend to God and to be engaged with the world.

There is, however, more to change than taking seriously the context in which we church people live and the psychological difficulties we have of taking change on board, as important as both of those are. For the Christian there are also powerful spiritual matters at stake here. The world of the Christian faith is a world dominated by words; indeed the prime metaphor for Jesus as the Son of God is 'the Word', 'the Word made flesh'. And when you have settled on a way of speaking, which is also your way of thinking, the words you use take on a life and power of their own. Changing them is more than merely using one set of words rather than another; it indicates a change of mind and understanding. And Christians are terribly fearful of getting their words wrong – though they are not alone in that as arguments in the physical sciences, the social sciences and even in Parliament show. Christians, after all, have suffered and died and made others suffer and sometimes die for the words they used. And while some Christians are happy to say and understand, for instance, that the phrase 'Jesus is the Lamb of God' is a metaphorical way of speaking and is not literally true, they might get uncomfortable, perhaps even angry, if you say that the phrase 'Jesus is the Son of

God' is also a metaphorical way of speaking and not literally true.

So change is a spiritual matter as well as a psychological one, and that means that it touches the core of the Christian faith deeply. Because of the belief that God does not change, it is argued that our spirituality, faith and beliefs should not change either; they have been revealed to us once and for all and we need only accept them. These are all matters to which I will return.

Just before I turn to look at change in the New Testament, I want to tell you a joke that perfectly illustrates both perceptions about change in the Church, and about other matters as well. It comes, of course, from the television programme about the Vicar of Dibley. Two women clergy are sitting at a table, talking over coffee. The one says, 'Let me tell you a joke. How many Church of England clergymen does it take to change a light bulb?'

'I don't know', says the other, 'how many men does it take?'

'Change', replies the first, 'what do you mean – change?'

I am going to begin my exploration of change with a quick trot through the New Testament to hear a bit of what it has to say on the subject. I do this for two reasons. First, for some Christian people starting with the Bible is the only way to get a hearing. And second, I want to begin building my case for saying that change is not just an unfortunate part of the realities of life, or even an evil to be avoided, but that change is a theological necessity and a spiritual imperative.

As we have seen already, one of the key concepts in the New Testament arises from the word *metanoia*. We saw in Chapter 4 that most of the time it is translated as 'conversion', but that its primary meaning is 'a change of mind', which is almost always, in the New Testament, used in the context of 'repentance' – the kind of repentance that leads to a change away from a life of sin and towards following the ways of God or Christ.

This is a central New Testament concept, and quite important for understanding the dynamic of the Christian faith. The beginning of the Christian's engagement with God is change: change from being one kind of person to being another; change from following false gods to following the true God; change from one way of thinking to another. For many Christians this is seen as a one-off event: you are converted, you are changed. And in the context of my Baptist youth, it was an event you could date so that you could answer the question, 'When were you born again?'

This rather static understanding of *metanoia*, however, fails to register the other great movement to change in the New Testament: the change that comes along with the trump of doom. In St Paul's first letter to the somewhat truculent Christians in Corinth in the middle of the first century, he has a long passage about the resurrection from the dead – itself, of course, about a major change. In it he talks about the end of all things and writes this:

> Listen, I will tell you a mystery! We will not all die, but we will all be changed, in a moment, in the twinkling of an eye, at the last trumpet. For the trumpet will sound, and the dead will be raised imperishable, and we will be changed.
>
> (1 Corinthians 15.51–52)

Don't worry for the moment about what exactly St Paul is describing here and whether or not he was expecting the end of the world in his lifetime; that is not the issue. The main point for this discussion is that not only is the beginning of the Christian life about change, so is the end. The inner dynamic of the Christian faith is a movement from change to change. Change in the Christian scheme of things is a constant process in this life, and I can see no reason for it also not to be a constant process in the life to come.

That change *is* the dynamic of the Christian faith is also indicated by Jesus. Speaking to his disciples just before the awful climax of his ministry, John's Gospel records Jesus as saying:

I still have many things to say to you, but you cannot bear them now. When the Spirit of truth comes, he will guide you into all the truth, for he will not speak on his own, but will speak whatever he hears, and he will declare to you the things that are to come.

(John 16.12–13)

Being guided into truth seems a pretty good way of describing the need to change, and indicates to me, at any rate, that not to change is to stop growing into truth. Just as importantly, I think it also indicates that truth is not a static concept either. An idea or proposition is not, as popular preachers would have us believe, either true or not true. Sometimes things might well be true enough to be getting on with, truth for now. But I am anticipating something to which I want to come back later in this chapter.

There is one more bit of the New Testament I want to look at before we move on, which follows on from St Paul's notion that we will all be changed, and that is the notion that *metanoia* leads to a new creation, the beginning of the process of creating something new. In St Paul's second letter to those same truculent Christians in Corinth, he writes, 'So if anyone is in Christ, there is a new creation: everything old has passed away; see, everything has become new' (2 Corinthians 5.17). This simply reinforces the sense I have that the inner dynamic of the Christian faith is change: change from old to new, a new creation beginning.

The reason for briefly going through this material from the New Testament is to point to the fact that the case I am making – that change is normal, and a natural part of what it means to be a Christian – has a biblical grounding and is not something I've just plucked out of the air.

I now want to do something for which I am not qualified, and that is to drag a little more of my argument in favour of change from science. So a word of warning: I am not a scientist, and I do not pretend to know anything about the subjects I will mention. I do, however, like to listen to scientists – especially when they speak in the kind of English that the rest of us use. What follows is a little bit of what I have picked up from them.

I want to start with one of the most amazing lectures I have ever attended, some years ago now, at the Royal Institution in London. One of my parishioners invited my wife and me to an evening on 'Rock Mechanics'. Yes, I was stunned by the title as well. The format of the lectures is pretty well known. The lecturer is locked in a room for 20 minutes before the lecture so that they don't run away, as happened once, apparently, in the nineteenth century. At precisely 6.00 p.m., the door opens and, without any preliminaries, the lecturer walks in and begins. At precisely two minutes to 7.00 p.m. the lecturer stops and is led from the room. Our man on rock mechanics clearly spoke too quickly early on and was equally clearly waffling for the last couple of minutes. But apart from that, it was a real *tour de force*.

The burden of his argument was that far from being static things, there is constant movement and change within rocks, the most dead-seeming of inanimate objects. Of course the change is only just detectable, but it is there and it is measurable. He had become something of an expert on this because he was employed to use this knowledge to help in the extraction of oil.

The interest for me was that even with rocks you don't get away from change. Those wonderful landscapes you get in the mountains are not unchanging, but teeming with change not only because of external forces such as wind and weather, but also through the ways things are at an internal and microscopic level.

It is, however, from the biological sciences that I can take the best analogy. At a cellular level, things are changing in living organisms all the time. In fact all there is is change. Our bodies are never static: they are either changing and growing or changing and decaying. For living organisms to live is to change; not to change is to die.

There are, of course, more profound analogies to be drawn from the biological sciences. We only need to think about the place of change in evolutionary biology to see that change is not just important to individual organisms, but to whole species and their survival. We could look at the macro-environment and see the ways in which constant change has a profound effect not only on where that change takes place but also in the whole ecosystem, from the so-called butterfly effect through to the depletion of the ozone layer over the Antarctic. The point is that the world in which we live is one of constant change, and we human beings are no exception to it.

So from the way things are in the world in which we live, and which Christians like to think of as created and made holy by God, and from the inner dynamic of the Christian faith itself, we can begin to see that far from being an unpleasant problem to cope with, change is all there is. And the Christian faith cannot be an exception to this general rule. There is enough special pleading in Christian theology without special pleading about change.

At almost every step of the way in this chapter, we have bumped into the question of truth in this business of change. And God is the heart of the problem. Or, less polemically, our understanding of God is the heart of the problem. So it is to this question of truth, God and change that we need to turn. We begin with God.

We have seen already, even from 'Abide with me', that many Christians work on the assumption that whatever else may change God does not. St Augustine, in one of his prayers, would have us rest in the 'eternal changelessness' of God. Or in the letter to the Hebrews in the New Testament we hear Jesus described as 'the same yesterday and today and for ever' (Hebrews 13.8).

When we move on a century or two from the New Testament, and look at the intellectual life of the early Church, we see that thinking about God began to follow a variety of philosophical fashions, many of which were taken up with the notion of divine perfection. The idea of divine perfection often had its roots in mathematics and ethics. God is a perfect unity and, unlike human beings, is not subject to whims of passion or external forces of any kind. God is, in the words of the second-century theologian Justin Martyr, 'the unchanging, and eternal God, the begetter of all things' (1 *Apol.* 13).

One of the so-called attributes of God which brings much of this thought together is 'impassibility', an attribute that implies the moral perfection of God and is a property belonging to God alone. G. L. Prestige in his magisterial book *God in Patristic Thought*, summarizes impassibility like this:

God, says Clement (*strom.* 4.23, 151.1), is impassible, without anger and without desire. God is impassible and changeless, he repeats (*ecl. Proph.* 52.2); impassible and unalterable, says

Methodius (*de creat.* 4.1), and proceeds to defend the position that the act of creation involved no change in the being of God himself. It is clear that impassibility means not that God is inactive or uninterested, not that He surveys existence with Epicurean impassivity from the shelter of a meta-physical insulation, but that His will is deter-mined from within instead of being swayed from without. It safeguards the truth that the impulse alike in providential order and in redemption and sanctification comes from the will of God. If it were possible to admit that the impulse was wrung from Him either by the needs or by the claims of His creation, and that thus whether by pity or by justice His hand was forced, He could no longer be represented as absolute; He would be dependent on the created universe and thus at best only in possession of concurrent power.[1]

I've included that rather long quotation to give a sense of the roots of the problem Christians often have with change: change is what happens to pathetic creatures like you and me, but not to perfect beings like God.

Apart from the philosophical and theological nice-ties, the changelessness of God was seen as important for psycho-spiritual reasons as well. Human beings – who are changeable, fickle, limited and subject to forces beyond their control and, worst of all, subject to their own passions – need to be assured that at the heart of existence and reality there is a Being who is not fickle like them, who is not limited like them, who is not subject to external forces like them, who is dependable, just and passionless, who is changeless.

Christians, however, also hold that the eternal and unchanging God also makes himself known through and in his creation. God is seen to reveal Godself. Because God is this unchanging Being beyond our thought and imagining, so the revelation of this God – because it is from the unchanging God – is also thought to be unchanging, and unchangeable. God's revelation should be as dependable as God is. So the truth of that revelation should be unchanging too.

There is a certain philosophical neatness about this that has its attractions, and it bears some of the necessary psycho-spiritual weight as well; but these are views it is very difficult to sustain from the Bible, and perhaps even from experience. The Bible is full of stories about God being moved to love, anger, pity or revenge. The Bible has many instances of God changing his mind in reaction to events or to the prayers of his people. Indeed, the Christian faith was born out of a Jewish religion with an ancient and honourable tradition of entering into debate with God. But most of all, the Christian tradition has viewed the ultimate revelation of God as coming in the form of a genuine human being, subject like all other human beings to the context and vagaries of existence. Not only that, this revelation through this person was seen to change and develop much that had gone before and to present a new understanding of the truth about God and the relationship of God to God's people. The biblical tradition then sees truth and, to some extent God, as evolving, as developing, as dynamic.

The Church soon turned its back on this more dynamic understanding of truth and God. It took on philosophical insights and criteria for speaking about God, and placed the revelation of God and the truth about God into the constraints of this intellectual context. Change – either in understanding God or in understanding the truth of God's revelation – became a bad thing.

Now I realize that this is being a little simplistic and perhaps even a bit rude towards those for whom a philosophical viewpoint is both important and productive. But I have to say that it is not clear to me why the biblical insights need to be so fully abandoned, or why the Church should have decided that the philosophies current during the period when orthodox understandings were developed should be seen as normative for ever. Most of 2,000 years later we do not hold a Platonic or Aristotelian view of the world. Indeed we have reached a point, in Western cultures at any rate, where no overarching philosophical programme is seen to be viable, the problem of so-called postmodernism.

So the philosophical project of the early Church looks more and more irrelevant as a result. Change is needed. But change in a context where almost any half-baked idea will do as a basis for life and thought is difficult to welcome and almost impossible to manage. So to change, for some, is to be seen to give in to too many modern cultural and intellectual evils.

In his most recent books, *Tradition and Imagination* and *Discipleship and Imagination*,[2] David Brown, the Van Mildert Professor of Divinity at Durham University, has a long and thorough examination of these subjects, especially those of revelation and truth. Without trying to relate the somewhat dense arguments of 800 or more pages, he concludes that both revelation and truth are indeed dynamic and changing notions. Because he has a proper place for the imagination, he recognizes that truth cannot be limited to what is supposed to be factual or literal; the imaginative, even fictive articulation of truth is every bit, if not more, important. And however much theologians and church people might protest, the history of the Church and theology is full of changing understandings of truth, even changing understandings of God and Jesus.

Importantly, however, Brown does not see this as a progressive thing, as if we might have 'more' truth, as it were, than previous generations. Imagination allows and empowers us to go back into the tradition to recover truths long buried, or to follow different

trajectories of thought into new areas or to accommo-
date new understandings. But in the Christian tradition, truth is not just what is true for *me* – which is the
modern problem – truth is what is true for *us* and what
enables us to be faithful to God and to the trajectories
of faith. This is why, for example, the Church can
decide to ordain women to ministerial priesthood. Not
because it is in the Bible or the 'unbroken' tradition of
the Church (which it is not), but because it is not difficult to take the example of Christ in his dealings with a
whole range of people and work out a trajectory from
them that makes it possible, even necessary, to allow
the women in.

Before I move on from this discussion to begin
drawing this chapter and the book to a close, I would
like briefly to comment on the one great problem that I
have skirted so far in this discussion of change: Does
God change? To ask this question is to move into deep
waters – both philosophical and theological – and there
is a need to move carefully.

In answering the question, a lot depends on where
you start. To start from a classical philosophical stand-
point is to rule out the question; of course God does
not change for God is not like us and is, therefore,
impassible, as we have already seen. But if we start
from a theological perspective the question might be
answered differently. Certainly on a surface reading of
the Old Testament God is seen to be interacting with

his people: being angered by their sin or stubbornness, being moved to pity or love by their plight, being persuaded out of a course of action by a righteous person, and so on. God, in the Old Testament, might be inscrutable, but not immovable.

The New Testament and subsequent Christian thinking about God hinges on how we view Jesus. In Jesus, God is seen to be acting in a new and decisive way in relation to his people. According to orthodox Christian belief, Jesus was God in human flesh, and the doctrine of the Trinity was developed to explain how God could remain God and still be incarnate in the human Jesus and with us now in the Holy Spirit. Because of the philosophical understandings at the time that the doctrine of the Trinity was developed, it was both a pretty static and a pretty distant understanding of God as Trinity: God may have become human, but God also lost nothing of the impassible attributes given to God in the process.

In recent decades a different kind of slant has been given to the doctrine of the Trinity, which gives God back something of the involvement with the life of creation that we get with God as portrayed in the Old Testament. The German Lutheran theologian Jürgen Moltmann wrote a seminal book on this subject called *The Crucified God*[3] in which he explored, among many other things, what the crucifixion of Jesus meant for God. In the book he argues that taking a Trinitarian understanding of God seriously means that God is indeed changed by his experience of the crucifixion of Jesus; God himself experiences godforsakenness, and is changed by the experience since it is, by definition, a new experience for God. We could also point to the incarnation, which was also a new experience for God, where humanity is taken up into the life of God and the life of God brought into the life of humanity. God does a new thing, and God is changed in the process.

Part of the problem here is one of language. As we have seen already, all of the great minds who have thought about God agree that human language is incapable of expressing anything true about God, for God is beyond the capacity of our language: everything we say not only falls short but is also, to some considerable extent, untrue. But in traditional and modern Christian theology, Christians have wanted to say that in Jesus we see something of the truth of God and can articulate it precisely because we see that truth out of our experience and in another human person. Therefore, as we have seen, Christians have also wanted, at the very least, to be able to say that God is Jesus Christlike. And in Jesus Christ we see a God who is capable of love and anger, who is moved to action by argument and compassion, who is stirred by the faith of others, who is anything but impassible. Now I realize that good Lutherans would say, 'But that is only God as God is revealed to us and not God as God is in

Godself', and I would have to agree. But if we want to take the notion that in Christ we see *something* of the truth about God – even if it is not the whole truth about God – then I find the notion that God can and does change pretty irresistible. And if God can change, then so must we.

I want to come back to the story from the Gospels, which we looked at briefly in Chapter 2, about the encounter Jesus had with a foreign woman. The story is from Matthew 15.21–28. In Chapter 2 I suggested that Jesus was clearly changed by this encounter. From ignoring the woman, to calling her a dog, he eventually moves to commending her for her faith. I think the course of his ministry is changed, and certainly the course of his thinking. Here, the one who is to be God for us is changed by the love, persistence, faith and humility of this foreign woman. No impassibility here; but God moved and changed by forces external to himself.

If I was being less polite than I have been – which means I am just about to *be* less polite – I would say that many church people make a lot of frightened stuff and nonsense out of change. For all the wrong reasons many think that change will do them harm, when in fact change is all there is: change is the essence of life, and change is a part of the life of God. Temperamentally, I am a person who welcomes and indeed even encourages change; temperamentally, others are different. But that's too bad. Temperamentally I am also inclined to be lazy, rude and grumpy, but am not generally allowed to get away with it and am often told by my long-suffering wife simply to grow up. And just because religion and God is involved in this discussion about change, we church people are not exempt from taking it seriously, no matter how temperamentally difficult we find it. We, too, as church people, need to grow up.

I do not want, however, to end on such a grumpy and self-indulgent note. While the dynamic for change in all of life may be irresistible, it does not follow that all change is good, and this is a good reason for at least questioning change, if not for resisting it. But this is where we also run into more than logic, if I can put it that way. Whether or not change is good or for the better may not just be a matter of argument, but of taste. This is why changes in liturgy are often such fraught affairs in the Church, because it's not just about the possible truth of what we say and pray, but it's also about whether or not we like it. No matter that its language is all but incomprehensible except to an ever-decreasing few, or that its theology is deeply suspect in places, lovers of the Prayer Book resist change like no others. Even not-quite-so-loved modern services are now viewed nostalgically by increasing numbers of people who have known only that, as liturgical change continues apace. Much of the resistance to change in worship has nothing to do with theology, communication or accessibility; it's largely a matter of taste.

This is also a place where our thoughts about truth come back into play. David Brown, among others, would argue that it is precisely in the conflict over change that we begin to discover something about truth. If I may be allowed to put it in a polemical way, truth has always been a matter of consensus. If you see things in one way and I see things in another, it may not be that one of us is right and the other wrong. It may be that in the conflict we have, we discern a greater or a different truth together. Truth is not something 'out there' waiting to be discovered, like the truth about aliens in *The X Files*. As Mulder and Scully discover, truth is many-layered and richly textured and a great deal depends on where you stand when you look at things. And no matter how much one might wish to contest this view when it comes to science or mathematics, though I still think it holds, it is ever so true of our understanding not only of God, but also of ourselves. The deepest truths to be known in the universe are not about cosmology and black holes and dark matter; the deepest truths are those of the human heart and mind, and these are sometimes the most difficult truths to grasp and articulate.

I've tried to explore change in this chapter from a number of perspectives, and as a way of helping us see what it means to attend to God and be the Body of Christ. I suppose that the whole burden of my argument is that change is normal, natural, a sign of life and generally a good thing and nothing of which to be frightened. Perhaps accepting that change is normal, natural and inevitable may be some comfort to those who are frightened of change and who think it is a bad thing, perhaps even evil.

In whatever way we might view change or feel about it, there is no getting away from it. In the same ways that humans have adapted to the realities of their physical environment over the millennia, perhaps it is also time for us – especially those of us in the churches – to learn to adapt to the realities of our intellectual and spiritual environment as well. The only other option is intellectual and spiritual extinction.

All of this is of great relevance to what it means to be the Body of Christ in the world. If we really are to attend to the God who is God of all creation, then we need to be prepared to change and be changed. If we are going to explore our faith with honesty and integrity, then we need to be prepared to change and be changed. If we are to engage with the world in any meaningful way, then we must be prepared to change and be changed. If we are to be the Body of Christ in and for the world, then we must be prepared to change and be changed as we follow the Spirit of God in the world.

To follow God, to become Christ-like, to be Christ for the world requires enormous changes – in us, in our Church and in our mission. Things can never again be the way they were. Saying that is only to acknowledge the real inner dynamic of the Christian life and faith. If we want our spirituality to be real, if we want our faith to matter in the world, if we want to work for the kingdom God seeks for the world, then we must change, and change again. And again. World without end.

Notes

CHAPTER 5

1 Rowan Williams' discussion of the language religious people use in *Writing in the Dust* (London, Hodder & Stoughton, 2002) should be required reading for all Christians as we think about how we engage with the world and relate to our culture.

2 London, Hodder & Stoughton, 1983.

CHAPTER 6

1 *Summa of Christian Teaching*, I, 30, as translated and quoted in Mary T. Clark, *An Aquinas Reader* (London, Hodder & Stoughton, 1972), pp. 136–7.

2 *Metaphor and Religious Language*. Oxford, OUP, 1985.

3 *God, Christ and the World*. London, SCM Press, 1969, p. 37.

CHAPTER 7

1 London, SPCK, 1952, p. 7.
2 *Tradition and Imagination*. Oxford, OUP, 1999; *Discipleship and Imagination*. Oxford, OUP, 2000.
3 London, SCM Press, 1975.